Abraham H. Cannon

**Questions and Answers on the Book of Mormon**

Designed and prepared especially for the use of the Sunday schools in Zion

Abraham H. Cannon

**Questions and Answers on the Book of Mormon**
*Designed and prepared especially for the use of the Sunday schools in Zion*

ISBN/EAN: 9783337297725

Printed in Europe, USA, Canada, Australia, Japan

Cover: Foto ©Lupo / pixelio.de

More available books at **www.hansebooks.com**

# QUESTIONS AND ANSWERS

ON THE

# BOOK OF MORMON.

---

*DESIGNED AND PREPARED ESPECIALLY FOR THE USE OF*
*THE SUNDAY SCHOOLS IN ZION,*

## BY A. H. CANNON.

PUBLISHED AT THE

Juvenile Instructor Office,

Salt Lake City, Utah.,

1886.

# PREFACE.

IT affords us very much pleasure to be able to present this little volume to the public at this time. A constant demand for a work of this kind induced us to undertake its preparation, and that it might be sufficiently cheap in price as to place it within the reach of all, we were necessarily compelled to do but poor justice to the sacred record upon which it treats. We have endeavored, however, to touch upon the most important items of history and doctrine, so that by a study of the lessons herein contained a good idea may be obtained of the Book of Mormon.

The importance of a careful study of writings so fraught with historical and religious truths as the volume translated by the Prophet Joseph Smith, cannot be over-restimated. And our most earnest desire will be gratified if these questions and answers can but induce the young people of Zion to search with greater diligence for the valuable truths contained in the revelations of ancient and modern times, all of which are given the Latter-day Saints for their instruction.

THE PUBLISHERS.

# CONTENTS

## CHAPTER I.

## CHAPTER II.

## CHAPTER III.

## CHAPTER IV.

## CHAPTER V.

## CHAPTER VI.

## CHAPTER VII.

## CHAPTER VIII.

## CHAPTER IX.

## CHAPTER X.

# CHAPTER XI.

# CHAPTER XII.

# CHAPTER XIII.

# CHAPTER XIV.

# CHAPTER XV.

# CHAPTER XVI.

# THE BOOK OF MORMON.

## CHAPTER I.

THE BOOK OF MORMON—WHAT IT IS—WHERE HIDDEN—
WHEN AND BY WHOM OBTAINED—THE TRANSLATION
OF THE PLATES—DELIVERY OF PLATES.

1 Q. WHAT is the Book of Mormon?
A. The sacred history of ancient America.

2 Q. By whom was it written?
A. A succession of ancient prophets who inhabited the continent.

3 Q. On what was it written?
A. On plates which had the appearance of gold.

4 Q. Of what size were the plates?
A. About eight inches long, seven inches wide, and not quite as thick as common tin, the whole being about six inches in thickness.

5 Q. How were they bound?
A. Together in a volume, as the leaves of a book, being fastened at one edge by three rings running through each.

6 Q. What kind of characters were engraved on the plates?
A. Reformed Egyptian characters were found on both sides of each plate.

7 Q. Where was the record obtained?
A. From the hill Cumorah, Ontario County, in the state of New York.

8 Q. By whom?
A. Joseph Smith.

9 Q.   When?

   A.   On the morning of September 22nd, 1827.

10 Q.   How did he learn where they were?

   A.   He was told by an angel of the Lord, four years previously.

11 Q.   In what were they concealed?

   A.   A stone box strongly cemented together which was placed beneath the soil.

12 Q.   How large was the box?

   A.   Sufficiently large to admit of a breast-plate, such as was used by the ancient warriors and the Urim and Thummim to be placed in it, together with the plates.

13 Q.   How were the plates placed?

   A.   Upon three small pillars of cement which arose from the bottom of the box.

14 Q.   In what condition was the box and its contents found?

   A.   When first visited, in 1823, a small part of the crowning stone was visible above the ground, but when opened it was seen that no dampness had penetrated to the interior of the box.

15 Q.   After Joseph Smith had found the place, opened the box and was viewing the contents, who appeared to him?

   A.   The angel Moroni who had previously visited him, and who was surrounded by the glory of God.

16 Q.   Did any other personage appear to him?

   A.   Yes, the prince of darkness, with his hosts.

17 Q.   Why was he shown the two powers?

   A.   That he might thereafter know them and not be influenced or overcome by the evil one.

18 Q.   What did the angel say the plates contained besides the history of an ancient people?

   A.   The fulness of the everlasting gospel.

19 Q.   Why were these things shown and told to Joseph Smith?

   A.   Because he was chosen to translate the characters and found, under God, the great latter-day work.

20 Q. When the interpretation was completed to whom was the book to be sent?

   A. To every nation, kindred, tongue and people under the whole heaven.

21 Q. What was to follow?

   A. The Priesthood should be given to some, the gospel be preached, and numerous blessings be conferred.

22 Q. Was that all?

   A. No, persecution should increase as the work progressed.

23 Q. How was the translator to be aided in his work?

   A. By the gift of God and the use of the Urim and Thummim.

24 Q. What was the Urim and Thummim?

   A. It consisted of two transparent stones, clear as crystal, set in the two rims of a bow.

25 Q. By whom was it used anciently?

   A. Persons called seers.

26 Q. For what purpose?

   A. To receive revelation of things distant, or of things past or future.

27 Q. When was the translation of the plates commenced?

   A. In December, 1827.

28 Q. At what place?

   A. Harmony, Pennsylvania.

29 Q. Who was Joseph Smith's first scribe?

   A. Martin Harris.

30 Q. To whom were some of the characters shown when translated?

   A. To Professor Anthon of New York.

31 Q. Who was Professor Anthon?

   A. A man deeply learned in both ancient and modern languages.

32 Q. Why were the characters sent to him?

   A. That the words of the Prophet Isaiah might be fulfilled, as found in his twenty-ninth chapter.

33 Q. Repeat the eleventh and twelfth verses of this chapter.

A. "And the vision of all is become unto you as the words of a book that is sealed, which men deliver to one that is learned, saying, Read this, I pray thee; and he saith, I cannot; for it is sealed; and the Book is delivered to him that is not learned, saying, Read this, I pray thee; and he saith, I am not learned."

34 Q. Who is meant by "him that is not learned?"

A. Joseph Smith.

35 Q. Who wrote for Joseph in 1829?

A. Oliver Cowdery.

36 Q. When was the translation completed?

A. In the year 1829.

37 Q. Were all of the plates translated?

A. No.

38 Q. Why not?

A. Because a part was sealed and only the open part was to be given to the world at that time.

39 Q. When the translation was finished to whom were the plates delivered?

A. An angel of the Lord.

40 Q. When was the first edition of the Book of Mormon printed?

A. In the year 1830.

## CHAPTER II.

WRITER OF THE BOOK OF MORMON—WHEN HIDDEN—WIT-NESSES OF THE BOOK—THE JAREDITES—WHO THEY WERE—A SECOND RACE—THE REMNANTS—THE PROM-ISES TO THE INDIANS—THEIR PREPARATION.

1 Q. WHY is the translation called the Book of Mormon?

A. Because an ancient prophet named Mormon compiled an abridgment from the records of his forefathers.

2 Q. Is the Book of Mormon a full copy of these ancient records?

**A.** No, only a small part of them.

3 **Q.** What was done with these numerous records?

**A.** They were hid up in the hill Cumorah.

4 **Q.** To whom did Mormon deliver his writings?

**A.** To his son Moroni.

5 **Q.** What did Moroni do with them?

**A.** He finished the record up to the time when the people of God were overcome by the wicked, when he hid them also in the hill Cumorah.

6 **Q.** In what year was this?

**A.** In the four hundred and twentieth year of the Christian era.

7 **Q.** How long, then, did these plates remain concealed in the ground, before delivered to Joseph Smith?

**A.** About fourteen hundred and ten years.

8 **Q.** Was the translator the only person who saw these plates?

**A.** No.

9 **Q.** Name three others who saw them.

**A.** Oliver Cowdery, David Whitmer and Martin Harris.

10 **Q.** Who showed them the plates?

**A.** "An angel of God."

11 **Q.** Who commanded them to bear record of the same?

**A.** The Lord.

12 **Q.** Where is the testimony of these three witnesses to be found?

**A.** At the front part of the Book of Mormon.

13 **Q.** Were these the only persons who saw the plates?

**A.** No, there were eight others.

14 **Q.** Name them.

**A.** Christian Whitmer, Jacob Whitmer, Peter Whitmer, Jun., John Whitmer, Hiram Page, Joseph Smith, Sen., Hyrum Smith and Samuel H. Smith.

15 **Q.** By whom were the plates shown them?

**A.** By the translator, Joseph Smith, Jun.

16 **Q.** What did they testify concerning the appearance of the plates?

**A.** That they had the appearance of gold and seemed to be of ancient work and curious workmanship.

17 Q.   Where can their testimony be found?

A.   On the same page with that of the three witnesses.

18 Q.   While these men testified that they saw and handled the plates, is there any testimony that they were correctly translated by the gift and power of God?

A.   Yes, the three witnesses testify to this?

19 Q.   Anyone else?

A.   Yes, every faithful Latter-day Saint.

20 Q.   To whom is the Book of Mormon written?

A.   To the Lamanites, and also to Jew and Gentile.

21 Q.   Who are the Lamanites?

A.   A remnant of the House of Israel whom we often call Indians.

22 Q.   How was the record written?

A.   By way of commandment and also by the spirit of prophecy and revelation.

23 Q.   What does the Book of Mormon contain?

A.   A history of the various peoples who inhabited tl is land from early times until the beginning of the fifth century of the Christian era.

24 Q.   How many distinct races occupied this land anciently as mentioned in the Book of Mormon?

A.   Two.

25 Q.   What was the first or more ancient race called?

A.   Jaredites.

26 Q.   Who were they?

A.   A people whose forefathers were led from the Tower of Babel, at the time of the confusion of tongues, to America.

27 Q.   From whence came the second race?

A.   Jerusalem.

28 Q.   Who were they?

A.   Israelites.

29 Q.   When did they leave Jerusalem?

A.   About six hundred years before Christ.

30 Q.   During whose reign?

A.   The reign of Zedekiah, king of Judah.

31 Q.   When did the first nation cease to exist?

A. About the time the Israelites came from Jerusalem.

32 Q. When was the principal nation of the second race destroyed?

A. Towards the close of the fourth century.

33 Q. Who and where are the remainder?

A. The American Indians on this continent.

34 Q. Will this latter remnant ever be totally destroyed from the earth?

A. No.

35 Q. Why not?

A. Because God has made great promises to their forefathers concerning the work they should do.

36 Q. When were they to do this work?

A. In the latter days.

37 Q. Are they making preparations for this labor?

A. Yes.

38 Q. In what way?

A. By receiving the gospel and cultivating the arts of peace instead of those of war.

39 Q. What color are these people at the present time?

A. Reddish brown, though they are called "Red men."

40 Q. How came they to be of this color?

A. Through the curse pronounced upon them.

-----•◆•-----

## CHAPTER III.

LEHI'S VISION—DEPARTURE FROM JERUSALEM—THE RIVER LAMAN—THE VALLEY LEMUEL—SONS RETURN TO JERUSALEM—THE BRASS PLATES—HOW THEY WERE OBTAINED—ZORAM.

1 Q. WHOSE writings are found in the first part of the Book of Mormon?

A. Those of Nephi.

2 Q. Who was his father?

A. Lehi, who was a descendant of Manasseh, the son of Joseph, who was sold into Egypt.

3 Q.  How many brothers did he have older than himself, and what were their names?
A.  Three, Laman, Lemuel and Sam.

4 Q.  In what language did Nephi make his record?
A.  In that of his father, which consisted of the learning of the Jews, and the language of the Egyptians.

5 Q.  Who visited Jerusalem in the commencement of the first year of the reign of Zedekiah?
A.  Many prophets of God.

6 Q.  For what purpose?
A.  To warn the people to repent or their city would be destroyed.

7 Q.  Who was called from among the inhabitants of Jerusalem to lift a warning voice?
A.  Lehi.

8 Q.  How was he made acquainted with what was to happen?
A.  He was shown it in a vision.

9 Q.  Of what did he testify?
A.  Of the wickedness of the people, the downfall of Jerusalem, the coming of the Messiah and the redemption of the world.

10 Q.  How was his testimony received by the Jews?
A.  They mocked and sought to slay him.

11 Q.  Was the Lord satisfied with what he did?
A.  Yes, and blessed him.

12 Q.  How did Lehi escape from his enemies?
A.  The Lord commanded him in a dream to take his family and depart into the wilderness.

13 Q.  What did Lehi take with him into the wilderness besides his family?
A.  Nothing but provisions and tents.

14 Q.  What did he leave behind?
A.  His house, land, gold, silver and precious things.

15 Q.  What large body of water did he first reach?
A.  The Red Sea.

16 Q.  After three days' travel in the wilderness where did Lehi pitch his tent?

A. In a valley and by the side and near the mouth of a river which emptied into the Red Sea.

17 Q. What names did Lehi give to the river and valley?

A. To the river Laman, and to the valley Lemuel.

18 Q. In viewing the river and where it emptied, what did he say to Laman?

A. "O that thou mightest be like unto this river continually running into the fountain of all righteousness."

19 Q. What did he say to Lemuel?

A. "O that thou mightest be like unto this valley, firm and steadfast, and immoveable in keeping the commandments of the Lord."

20 Q. Why did Lehi thus address his sons?

A. Because of their unbelief and murmurings.

21 Q. What course did Nephi pursue?

A. He sought to know the mind and will of God, and therefore did not rebel against his father.

22 Q. What promises were made to him if he should be faithful?

A. He should be prospered, be led to a land of promise and be made a ruler and teacher over his brethren.

23 Q. Whose counsel did Sam follow?

A. That of his father and his brother Nephi.

24 Q. In the the event that Laman and Lemuel should rebel against God, what was to follow?

A. A sore curse.

25 Q. How did Laman and Lemuel feel about Nephi being called to be their ruler and teacher?

A. It caused them much anger and trouble.

26 Q. Why was not the oldest son chosen for this position?

A. Because of his wickedness.

27 Q. While Lehi and his family were encamped by the Red Sea, who were called to return to Jerusalem?

A. Nephi and his brothers.

28 Q. Who gave them the command?

A. The Lord by means of a dream to their father.

29 Q. What was the object of their journey?

A. To obtain some brass plates which contained the record of the Jews and some genealogies.

30 Q. In whose possession were they?

A. Laban's.

31 Q. Why did the Lord desire Lehi to have them?

A. That the valuable knowledge they contained might be preserved for future generations.

32 Q. When the sons reached Jerusalem how was it decided which of them was to visit Laban?

A. They cast lots.

33 Q. Upon whom did the lot fall?

A. Laman.

34 Q. When Laman asked Laban for the plates how was he treated?

A. He was thrust out and his life was sought.

35. Q. When he came to his brethren how did they feel?

A. Very sorrowful, and the older ones desired to return to their father.

36 Q. Who urged them not to do so?

A. Nephi.

37 Q. How did Nephi feel about the commands of God?

A. That the Lord would give no command to His children which it would be impossible for them to fulfill.

38 Q. What was the result of his belief on this point?

A. He became a successful and great man.

39 Q. What plan did the brothers next adopt for obtaining possession of the plates?

A. They gathered up the valuable things they had left when they went into the wilderness, and sought to purchase them.

40 Q. Were they successful?

A. No.

41 Q. What did Laban do?

A. He thrust them out and sent his servants to slay them.

42 Q. Why?

A. Because he coveted their property.

43 Q. Did the brothers escape?

A. Yes, and hid in the cavity of a rock.

44 Q. What became of their property?

A. They had to leave it and it fell into Laban's hands.

45 Q. When they were in the cavity how did Laman and Lemuel feel?

A. They were angry and smote their younger brother.

46 Q. While they were smiting Nephi who appeared to them?

A. An angel of the Lord.

47 Q. What did he do?

A. He chided them for their wickedness.

48 Q. What did the angel promise them concerning Laban?

A. That the Lord would deliver him into their hands.

49 Q. Who next went to Jerusalem?

A. Nephi.

50 Q. When did he go?

A. By night.

51 Q. As he approached Laban's house whom did he see?

A. Laban, lying drunk on the ground.

52 Q. What did the Spirit constrain him to do?

A. To slay Laban.

53 Q. How did Nephi feel about it?

A. He shrank from the shedding of blood.

54 Q. Did Nephi follow the promptings of the Spirit?

A. Yes, and smote off Laban's head with his own sword.

55 Q. Why did the Spirit prompt this act?

A. Because Laban was a murderer at heart, and it was better that a wicked man should perish than that a nation should dwindle and perish in unbelief.

56 Q. After this act what did Nephi do?

A. He dressed himself in Laban's clothes and went to his treasury.

57 Q. How did he there obtain the plates?

A. Through Laban's servant who supposed it was his master commanding him.

58 Q. What did he then do?

A. He took the servant and the plates towards where his brethren were hid.

59 Q.  When the brothers saw the two persons coming, what did they suppose?

A.  That Nephi had been slain and Laban was now coming to destroy them.

60 Q.  What did they do?

A.  They started to flee but Nephi called them.

61 Q.  What was Laban's servant then about to do?

A.  He trembled and would have fled.

➤ 62 Q.  How did Nephi persuade him to go with them?

A. ˙ By promising him his freedom.

63 Q.  What was this servant's name?

A.  Zoram.

———— ◆●◆ ————

## CHAPTER IV.

SONS RETURN AGAIN TO JERUSALEM—ISHMAEL AND HIS FAMILY—NEPHI'S VISION—TRAVELS IN THE WILDERNESS—LIAHONA—ISHMAEL'S DEATH—LAMAN'S WICKED PLAN—BOUNTIFUL.

1 Q.  How did the parents of Nephi and his brethren feel when their sons returned to them?

A.  They rejoiced exceedingly.

2 Q.  What did they offer to the Lord?

A.  Sacrifice and burnt offerings.

ƒ 3 Q.  When Lehi examined the plates what did he find they contained?

A.  The five books of Moses, a record of the Jews, many valuable prophecies and Lehi's own genealogy.

4 Q.  When Lehi saw these things what did he do?

A.  He began to prophesy concerning his seed and the future of the plates.

5 Q.  What was the next mission given to Lehi's sons?

A.  To return again to Jerusalem.

6 Q.  For what?

A.  To bring Ishmael and his family into the wilderness.

7. Q.  What was the object of this?

A. That Lehi's sons might have wives.

8 Q. Were they successful in their mission?

A. Yes, for the Lord made Ishmael favorable.

9 Q. While the company were returning to the encampment of Lehi who rebelled?

* A. Laman, Lemuel, the two sons and two daughters of Ishmael, with their families.

10 Q. What did the rebellious ones desire to do?

A. To return to Jerusalem.

11 Q. As Nephi exhorted them to do right and to keep the commandments of God, what did they do?

A. They seized and bound him with cords.

12 Q. How was he released?

A. He prayed to God and the bands were loosened.

13 Q. When they sought to lay hands on him again, who plead with them to desist?

A. A daughter and son of Ishmael and their mother.

14 Q. What effect did their pleadings have?

A. It softened the hearts of the rebellious ones.

15 Q. Were they humble?

A. Yes, and asked Nephi's forgiveness.

16 Q. What were the feelings of Lehi concerning his sons after a dream or vision given him while in the valley of Lemuel?

A. He rejoiced concerning Nephi and Sam, but had fears about Laman and Lemuel.

17 Q. What did the family gather while here encamped?

A. Seeds of every kind.

18 Q. What remarkable vision was given Nephi while in this valley?

A. He saw the future of his seed and that of his brethren, the coming of the Savior, the rise and progress of the mother of harlots, or the false churches, the discovery of America, the final restoration of the Gospel and triumph of the Saints, and many other important events.

19 Q. Why was he shown these things?

A. Because of his faith, humility and integrity.

20 Q.  When the journey was to be continued how was it made known to Lehi?

  A.  By the voice of the Lord at night.

21 Q.  When Lehi went to the tent door in the morning what did he find?

  A.  A brass ball of curious workmanship.

22 Q.  What was this ball called?

  A.  Liahona, which interpreted means a compass.

23 Q.  Of what use was this ball?

  A.  One of the two spindles it contained pointed in the direction they should travel.

24 Q.  Was there anything visible upon these pointers?

  A.  Yes, a writing which gave them understanding concerning the ways of the Lord.

25 Q.  Was this writing always the same?

  A.  No, it changed according to their faith and diligence.

26 Q.  In what direction did the company next travel?

  A.  South by south-east.

27 Q.  How long did they journey at this time?

  A.  For the space of four days.

28 Q.  Where did they next camp?

  A.  At the place of Shazer.

29 Q.  What route did they next pursue?

  A.  South by south-east, in the most fertile parts of the desert.

30 Q.  What was the next cause for murmuring among the company?

  A.  The lack of food through the breaking of Nephi's bow.

31 Q.  Who engaged in it?

  A.  All of them.

32 Q.  How was the difficulty overcome?

  A.  By Nephi making a wooden bow with which he slew game.

33 Q.  Who died in a place called Nahom?

  A.  Ishmael.

34 Q.  What would be our estimate of Ishmael's character from the account we have of him?

A. That he was a patient, faithful and humble man.

35 Q. After Ishmael's death what plan did Laman propose?

A. That they should kill Lehi and Nephi and then return to Jerusalem.

36 Q. How was the plan frustrated?

A. By the chastening voice of the Lord.

37 Q. What direction was now taken?

A. An easterly one.

38 Q. Where was their next stopping place?

A. Bountiful, so called because of its much fruit and wild honey.

39 Q. By what sea?

A. Irreantum, meaning many waters.

40 Q. How many years did the travelers sojourn in the wilderness.

A. Eight.

---◆-◆-◆--- ---

# CHAPTER V.

NEPHI BUILDS A SHIP—JOURNEY UNDERTAKEN ON THE WATER—TROUBLE AT SEA—ARRIVE AT PROMISED LAND —LEHI'S INSTRUCTIONS TO SONS—HIS DEATH.

1 Q. What duty was assigned Nephi in the land Bountiful?

A. He was commanded to construct a ship.

2 Q. Who was to give him a pattern?

A. The Lord.

3 Q. For what was the ship to be used?

A. To convey the people across the waters.

4 Q. Who made light of Nephi's task?

A. His brethren, who called him a fool.

5 Q. When they would have laid hands on him to throw him in the sea, how were they restrained.

A. By the power of God which filled Nephi.

6 Q. How were they made to feel this power?

A. By Nephi stretching forth his hand unto them.

7 Q.  How did the shock received make them feel?
A.  Very humble and penitent.

8 Q.  Where did Nephi frequently go to pray and receive instruction.
A.  Into the mountain.

9 Q.  When the ship was finished what did the company take with them into it.
A.  Fruit, meat, honey and other provisions as well as seeds and the things which they had brought with them.

10 Q.  Of what two sons of Lehi do we here find mention as having been born in the wilderness?
A.  Jacob and Joseph.

11 Q.  What power moved the ship?
A.  The wind.

12 Q.  Was the voyage a peaceful one?
A.  No, a great and terrible tempest arose.

13 Q.  Why was this?
A.  Because God was displeased with the actions of some of the company.

14 Q.  Who were they?
A.  Laman, Lemuel, the sons of Ishmael and their wives.

15 Q.  What did they do?
A.  They bound Nephi with cords because he urged them to do right.

16 Q.  How long did they leave him bound?
A.  Four days.

17 Q.  What was the result when he was loosened?
A.  The compass worked and the storm ceased.

18 Q.  After traveling some days what land did they reach?
A.  The Promised Land.

19 Q.  Where does the Prophet Joseph Smith tell us they landed?
A.  On the coast of Chili in South America.

20 Q.  After landing to what did they turn their attention?
A.  To agriculture.

21 Q.  What kind of animals did they find on the land?
A.  Beasts of every kind.

22 Q. What kind of minerals?
A. All manner of ore.
23 Q. What did Lehi learn concerning Jerusalem shortly after his arrival on the promised land?
A. That it had been destroyed.
24 Q. How did he get the knowledge?
A. It was given him in a vision.
25 Q. What were his feelings when this event was revealed to him.
A. He praised God for his deliverance.
26 Q. Who did he predict should inherit this land?
A. His seed and those whom God should lead out of other countries.
27 Q. What kind of a land was it to be?
A. A land of liberty.
28 Q. Had those who were led from Jerusalem all been faithful, who would have occupied the land?
A. They alone.
29 Q. Why are the remnants now driven before the white men?
A. Because of the unfaithfulness of their parents.
30 Q. Will it ever be thus?
A. No, a day of redemption will yet come for them.
31 Q. Of what great latter-day Prophet did Lehi make mention?
A. Joseph Smith.
32 Q. What was predicted concerning him?
A. That he should be a choice seer unto Lehi's posterity.
33 Q. What did Lehi do just before his death?
A. He called together his children.
34 Q. For what purpose?
A. To instruct and bless them.
35 Q. How alone could they claim the promised blessings?
A. By being faithful.
36 Q. If unfaithful what should follow?
A. Cursings.
37 Q. Were Lehi's instructions heeded by all after his death?

1*

A. No, wickedness began to be practiced not many days after his death.

38 Q. Who were they who turned to evil?

A. Laman, Lemuel and the sons of Ishmael.

39 Q. Against whom was their anger directed?

A. Nephi.

40 Q. What did they seek to do?

A. To kill him.

---

## CHAPTER VI

NEPHI SEPARATES FROM HIS BRETHREN—PLACE OF LOCA-
TION—PLATES ENTRUSTED TO JACOB—TWO SETS OF
PLATES—NEPHI'S DEATH—HIS CHARACTER—PEOPLE
PRACTICE INIQUITY—REPROVED BY JACOB—ZENOS'
WRITINGS.

1 Q. When the Lord saw the enmity of Nephi's brethren towards him what did He tell him to do?

A. To depart from them and go into the wilderness.

2 Q. Was he to go alone?

A. No, he was to take all who would go with him.

3 Q. Who did accompany him?

A. Nephi's family, Zoram and Sam and their families, and Jacob, Joseph, their sisters and others.

4 Q. What precious articles did Nephi take with him?

A. The records, ball and compass, and sword of Laban.

5 Q. After traveling many days what did they call the place where they located?

A. Nephi.

6 Q. In what direction is it probable they traveled?

A. Northward.

7 Q. What part of South America are we led to suppose the Land of Nephi embraced?

A. The country between the southern line of Ecuador and the northern line of Chili.*

---

* See Life of Nephi by George Q. Cannon, Page 88.

8 Q. What name did the followers of Nephi here adopt?
A. That of Nephites.

9 Q. What did Nephi here manufacture for the self-protection of his people?
A. Swords after the pattern of Laban's weapon.

10 Q. What kind of a building was here erected?
A. A temple.

11 Q. What name was given to the followers of Laman?
A. Lamanites.

12 Q. What was the curse sent upon them?
A. A dark skin.

13 Q. How long a time elapsed before wars arose between the two peoples?
A. Within forty years after leaving Jerusalem.

14 Q. What people were blessed of God?
A. The Nephites.

15 Q. How long did they continue to be thus favored?
A. As long as they kept God's commandments.

16 Q. What course did Jacob and Joseph pursue?
A. A righteous one.

17 Q. To whom did Nephi deliver his small plates upon which he had engraved so many valuable items?
A. To his brother Jacob.

18 Q. How long was this after they left Jerusalem?
A. Fifty-five years.

19 Q. What was to be engraved on these plates?
A. An account of the ministry and the more precious part of the prophecies.

20 Q. Where was the history of the people to be kept?
A. On other plates which Nephi had made.

21 Q. When Nephi began to grow old what did he do?
A. He anointed a man to be king and ruler over his people.

22 Q. What were the successors to Nephi in the rulership called?
A. Second Nephi, third Nephi, etc., no matter what their names might be.

23 Q. Why was this custom adopted?

    A.  Because the people loved Nephi greatly and desired that his name should be kept in remembrance.

24 Q.  Was the ruler in temporal affairs among the people also the presiding authority in spiritual matters?

    A.  Not always.

25 Q.  Did such a thing ever occur?

    A.  Yes; in Nephi both offices were united, but not again until Mosiah became king.

26 Q.  As a son what course did Nephi pursue?

    A.  He was dutiful and obedient.

27 Q.  As a man what qualities did he exhibit?

    A.  He was faithful to God, and kind, charitable and merciful towards all mankind.

28 Q.  What was the result of all this?

    A.  He was greatly blessed of God.

29 Q.  What should his example teach the children of the Latter-day Saints?

    A.  Faith in the Lord and obedience to His laws.

30 Q.  After Nephi's death what did his people begin to do?

    A.  To seek for wealth, and to get wives and concubines.

31 Q.  Was this proper?

    A.  No, it displeased the Lord.

32 Q.  Why.

    A.  Because their wealth made them proud, and they had not been commanded to have more than one wife.

33 Q.  Was the Lord opposed to their being rich?

    A.  Not as long as they did not set their hearts upon riches.

34 Q.  When is it proper for men to have more than one wife?

    A.  Only when God commands it.

35 Q.  Who admonished the people for their wickedness?

    A.  Jacob.

36 Q.  To what do we find the house of Isreal likened in the Book of Jacob?

    A.  To a tame olive tree which a man took and nourished in his vineyard.

37 Q.  What does the parable represent to us?

    A.  The trials and tribulations of the house of Israel.

38 Q.  From the words of what prophet is this parable taken?

    A.  Those of Zenos whose writings we do not have.

# CHAPTER VII.

SHEREM'S FALSE TEACHINGS—HIS FATE—PLATES HANDED
DOWN—LAND OF ZARAHEMLA—PEOPLE DISCOVERED—
KING BENJAMIN'S REIGN—HIS SONS—HIS WORDS TO
HIS PEOPLE—MOSIAH CHOSEN KING.

1 Q. After some years who came among the people preaching false doctrine?
A. Sherem.

2 Q. What was the result of his labors?
A. He gained many followers.

3 Q. What did he call the teachings of Jacob?
A. Blasphemy.

4 Q. Why did he say it was blasphemy?
A. Because he said it was impossible for anyone to know of Christ or things to come.

5 Q. When Jacob contended with him what did he desire?
A. A sign.

6 Q. What sign was given him?
A. He fell to the earth, and lost his strength, and had to be nourished for many days.

7 Q. The day before his death, of what did he testify to the people?
A. That he had sinned, and that Christ should come.

8 Q. When the multitude saw and heard these things what happened to them?
A. They were overcome by the power of God and fell to the earth.

9 Q. What success attended the efforts of the Nephites to reclaim the Lamanites?
A. Their efforts were in vain.

10 Q. When Jacob grew old to whom did he give the plates?
A. To his son Enos.

11 Q. How did Enos gain a knowledge of the truth?

A. By calling upon God in mighty prayer.

12 Q. Into whose hands did the plates pass after Enos?

A. Into those of his son Jarom.

13 Q. What is his testimony concerning the Nephites?

A. That they had waxed strong in the land, and were righteous.

14 Q. How long was this after leaving Jerusalem?

A. Two hundred years.

15 Q. What of the Lamanites at this time?

A. They were even more numerous than the Nephites, but were wicked.

16 Q. Who was the next possessor of the plates?

A. Omni, Jarom's son.

17 Q. Who was it that filled up the small plates of Nephi?

A. Amaleki.

18 Q. To whom did he deliver the plates?

A. To king Benjamin.

19 Q. Why did he do this?

A. Because he had no posterity of his own, and he knew this man to be upright.

20 Q. While Mosiah, father of Benjamin, was king whither were he and his people led?

A. Into the land of Zarahemla.

21 Q. Why did the people thus emigrate?

A. Because the Lord commanded it.

22 Q. On arriving in this land what did they find?

A. A people.

23 Q. Whence had they come?

A. From Jerusalem.

24 Q. At what time?

A. When Zedekiah was carried captive into Babylon.

25 Q. In what condition were they when found by Mosiah?

A. Their language had become corrupted and they had fallen into unbelief.

26 Q. What did Mosiah cause to be done?

A. He caused them to be taught in his language.

27 Q. What became of this people?

A. They united with the people of Mosiah.

28 Q. How did Mosiah gain a knowledge of Coriantumr and his people?

A. From the engravings on a large stone which was brought to him.

29 Q. Who succeeded Mosiah as king?

A. His son Benjamin.

30 Q. Who sought to obtain power over the Nephites during Benjamin's reign?

A. The Lamanites.

31 Q. What was the result of the battle?

A. The Lamanites were driven from the land.

32 Q. What kind of a man was Benjamin?

A. A righteous one.

33 Q. What were the names of his three sons?

A. Mosiah, Helorum and Helaman.

34 Q. How were they taught by their father?

A. In the ways of the Lord.

35 Q. Which of the three sons was chosen to be king and to take charge of the plates and other valuable articles?

A. Mosiah.

36 Q. How did king Benjamin proclaim this fact to his people?

A. He had them gather together at the temple.

37 Q. Were they inside the building?

A. No, it was too small to contain all.

38 Q. What arrangement was made?

A. The people camped about the building and the king had a tower built from which to address them.

39 Q. Could all hear?

A. No.

40 Q. What did he therefore cause to be done?

A. His words to be written and sent among the people.

41 Q. Of whom did the king prophesy?

A. Of the Savior who was to come.

42 Q. And what did he urge his people to do?

A. To be true to the Lord their God.

43 Q. What effect did his words have?

A. The fear of the Lord was upon the people and they fell to the earth.

44 Q. After they had cried for mercy and forgiveness, how did they feel?

A. They were filled with the joy and peace of the Holy Spirit.

45 Q. How were they told to retain this Spirit?

A. By doing right from day to day.

46 Q. What covenant did the people make after king Benjamin had finished speaking.

A. That they would serve the Lord.

---

## CHAPTER VIII.

MOSIAH'S REIGN—AMMON'S VISIT TO LEHI-NEPHI—LIMHI AND HIS PEOPLE—ZENIFF'S RECORD—THE PROPHET ABINADI—HIS LABORS AND PROPHECIES—HIS DEATH.

1 Q. How old was Mosiah when he began to reign?

A. Thirty years.

2 Q. How many years was this from the time Lehi left Jerusalem?

A. Four hundred and seventy-six.

3 Q. What course did Mosiah pursue?

A. He walked in the ways of the Lord.

4 Q. How did he gain a livelihood?

A. He tilled the earth so as not to be a burden to his people.

5 Q. After three years whom did Mosiah permit to go up to the land of Lehi-Nephi?

A. Sixteen of their strong men.

6 Q. Who was their leader?

A. Ammon, a descendant of Zarahemla.

7 Q. What was the object of this journey?

A. To learn something about a people who had left the land of Zarahemla some time before.

8 Q. After traveling forty days and pitching their tents, who went down into the land of Nephi?

A. Ammon, Amaleki, Helem and Hem.

9 Q. When they met the king's guard how were they treated?

A. They were bound and cast into prison.

10 Q. After being in prison two days, before whom were they taken?

A. Before the king, Limhi.

11 Q. Who did the king say he was?

A. A son of Noah, who was a son of Zeniff, who came from Zarahemla.

12 Q. When permitted to speak what did Ammon tell the king?

A. That he had come to inquire concerning the people whom Zeniff had led from Zarahemla.

13 Q. What effect did Ammon's words have upon the king?

A. They made him exceeding glad.

14 Q. What did he order done?

A. Ammon and his brethren released and the remainder of the company brought into the city from the place where they were camped.

15 Q. What was one reason of the king's rejoicing?

A. Because he hoped through the Nephites to be released from his bondage to the Lamanites.

16 Q. What tribute were he and his people paying to the Lamanites?

A. One half of all they had or possessed.

17 Q. What did they recognize as the cause of this bondage?

A. Their own wickedness.

18 Q. What did the king order brought for Ammon to read?

A. The plates containing the record of his people.

19 Q. After Ammon had finished them what did the king desire him to do further?

A. To translate the engravings on other twenty-four golden plates.

20 Q. Where had these been obtained?

A. They had been found in the wilderness.

21 Q. By whom?

A. By forty-three of Limhi's people whom he had sent out to find the people of Zarahemla.

22 Q. What else did they discover where the plates were found?

A. Bones of men and beasts, ruins of buildings, breast-plates, swords, etc.

23 Q. Who did Ammon say could translate the engravings?

A. The king of the people of Zarahemla.

24 Q. By what means?

A. Things called interpreters, known also to us as the Urim and Thummim, which were a gift from God.

25 Q. When could these be used?

A. Only when God commanded.

26 Q. In Zeniff's record what do we learn was the cause of his leaving Zarahemla?

A. His over-zeal to possess the land of his fathers.

27 Q. When he and his followers came to the king of the Lamanites what places were promised them?

A. The lands of Lehi-Nephi and Shilom.

28 Q. What object did the king have in giving these?

A. To bring the people into bondage.

29 Q. How long did they remain in peace?

A. For twelve years only.

30 Q. What was the result of the attack of the Lamanites upon them?

A. The Lord gave Zeniff and his people strength to defeat them.

31 Q. What did Zeniff teach his people to do?

A. To be industrious, and to serve the Lord.

32 Q. Who succeeded Zeniff as king?

A. His son Noah.

33 Q. What kind of a man was he?

A. A very wicked, impure man.

34 Q. What tax did he place upon the people for the support of himself, his wives, concubines and wicked priests?

A. One-fifth of all they possessed.

35 Q. When the king and his people began to be very wicked who was sent to warn them?

A. The prophet Abinadi.

36 Q. What did he tell them would happen if they did not repent?

A. They should be brought into bondage to their enemies.

37 Q. After the first warning of Abinadi how long before he visited them again?

A. Two years, when he came in disguise.

38 Q. What did he now predict?

A. Most terrible judgments upon king and people.

39 Q. What was the effect of his words?

A. It made the people angry and they took him bound before the king.

40 Q. When questioned what replies did he make?

A. Such as confounded his opponents.

41 Q. After Abinadi had partly finished speaking what did the priests seek to do?

A. To lay hands on him that they might slay him.

42 Q. How did he withstand them?

A. With the Spirit of the Lord that was upon him.

43 Q. When his testimony was given what became of him?

A. He was seized, bound, and cast into prison.

44 Q. After three days what punishment did he suffer?

A. He was brought before the king and accused of saying that God should come down among men.

45 Q. When he refused to deny his testimony who was inclined to release him?

A. King Noah, because he feared his word.

46 Q. Who opposed his release?

A. The priests.

47 Q. What was, therefore, done with him?

A. He was scourged and burned.

48 Q. How did he die?

A. With fortitude, bearing his testimony.

# CHAPTER IX.

Alma's Conversion—He Preaches and Converts Many —King Noah Sends an Army to Slay Alma and Followers—Escape in Wilderness—Wars Between Lamanites and Noah's People—Noah's Death— His People Escape.

1 Q. Who became convinced of the truth of Abinadi's words?

A. A young man named Alma.

2 Q. From whom was he descended?

A. From Nephi.

3 Q. When he heard the command of the king to seize and imprison Abinadi what did he do?

A. He plead that he might be released.

4 Q. What did the king order done with Alma?

A. He was cast out and servants were sent to slay him.

5 Q. How did he escape?

A. By hiding.

6 Q. After repenting of his sins what did Alma do?

A. He went privately among the people and taught them the words of Abinadi.

7 Q. Where did those go who believed his words?

A. To Mormon, on the borders of a land which was at times infested by wild beasts.

8 Q. Why did they go there?

A. That Alma, who hid himself there during the day, might teach them.

9 Q. What were they here taught?

A. The first principles of the gospel.

10 Q. From whom did Alma receive his commission to baptize?

A. From the Lord.

11 Q. How was the first baptism performed?

A. Alma took Helam with him into the waters of Mormon, and, after uttering a prayer, both were buried in the water.

12 Q. Were the subsequent baptisms performed in the same manner?

A. Yes, except that Alma was only immersed the once.

13 Q. What number received this ordinance?

A. Two hundred and four.

14 Q. When organized, what were they called?

A. The Church of God, or the Church of Christ.

15 Q. How many priests did Alma ordain?

A. One to every fifty of their number.

16 Q. What was their duty?

A. To teach the things pertaining to the kingdom of God.

17 Q. How did they do with their means?

A. They imparted one to the other that the needs of all might be supplied.

18 Q. When the king discovered this movement what did he do?

A. He sent his army to destroy these converts.

19 Q. How did Alma and his people escape?

A. They departed into the wilderness.

20 Q. When there was division among king Noah's people, who was it sought to kill him?

A. Gideon.

21 Q. How did the king escape death?

A. By begging for his life and saying that the Lamanites were coming upon them.

22 Q. When Noah and his people fled and were overtaken by their enemies, what did the king advise the men to do?

A. To leave their wives and children and seek safety themselves.

23 Q. What did those do who chose to remain with the helpless ones?

A. They caused their fair daughters to plead with the Lamanites.

24 Q.  What effect did this have?

A.  It softened the hearts of the savages and they spared them.

25 Q.  On what conditions were the conquered allowed to return and possess the land?

A.  By paying one-half of their possessions as tribute.

26 Q.  What became of Noah and his priests?

A.  He was burned to death by some of his own followers and his priests fled into the wilderness.

27 Q.  Who succeeded him as a ruler?

A.  His son Limhi, a just man.

28 Q.  What caused the next disturbance between the two peoples?

A.  The seizure of twenty-four Lamanite maidens by the priests of Noah, who had fled.

29 Q.  Why should this make feelings against Limhi?

A.  Because the Lamanites supposed that his people had done this.

30 Q.  What was the result of the battle?

A.  The Lamanites were defeated and their king was wounded and captured.

31 Q.  When matters were explained to him how did he pacify his people?

A.  By going with the unarmed Nephites and pleading for them.

32 Q.  What was the result of subsequent battles with the Lamanites?

A.  Limhi's people were defeated.

33 Q.  What treatment did they receive?

A.  They were afflicted with heavy tasks and burdens.

34 Q.  How did they find relief?

A.  Only by humbling themselves before God.

35 Q.  By whom had such afflictions been predicted?

A.  Abinadi.

36 Q.  When Ammon and his brethren came to them, what was it the study of Limhi's people to do?

A.  To effect their escape.

37 Q.  How was this done?

A. By leaving in the night with all they owned.

38 Q. How did they pass the guards whom the Lamanites had placed to watch them?

A. These had become drunken with the tribute of wine which Gideon had paid for Limhi's people.

39 Q. Whither did Limhi and his people go?

A. To Zarahemla.

---

## CHAPTER X.

LAMANITES CONQUER LIMHI'S PEOPLE—AMULON MADE RULER—HIS CRUELTY—PEOPLE ESCAPE—UNITE WITH NEPHITES—CONVERSION OF YOUNG ALMA AND THE KING'S SONS—JUDGES CHOSEN—NEHOR'S APOSTASY AND DEATH—WAR.

1 Q. After Alma and his converts had fled into the wilderness what did they desire Alma to become?

A. Their king.

2 Q. What was Alma's advice?

A. That they should not seek for a king.

3 Q. What position did Alma hold?

A. That of High Priest and leader.

4 Q. What was the name of the land and city where they settled?

A. Helam.

5 Q. Were they permitted to remain here in peace?

A. No, the Lamanites gained power over them,

6 Q. Whom did the victors appoint to rule over Alma and his people?

A. Amulon, who was leader of the priests of Noah, who had fled from the Lamanites, but whom those who persued Limhi, captured.

7 Q. How did he treat the people of Alma?

A. He placed heavy burdens upon them.

8 Q.  Why did the Lord permit this?

A.  To try the faith and patience of his people.

9 Q.  How did He first bring relief to them in answer to their prayers?

A.  By easing the burdens placed upon them.

10 Q.  How were they eventually delivered?

A.  By fleeing one morning when God caused a deep sleep to come upon their task-masters.

11 Q.  Whither did they go?

A.  To Mosiah and his people in Zarahemla.

12 Q.  When all these peoples were assembled, what did Mosiah cause to be done?

A.  The various records to be read.

13 Q.  Under what name did they unite?

A.  Nephites.

14 Q.  To what position did Mosiah call Alma?

A.  To hold authority over the Church.

15 Q.  With whom was the Church troubled at this time?

A.  Unbelievers.

16 Q.  Who were classed among these?

A.  The sons of Mosiah and one of Alma's sons who was named after himself.

17 Q.  As they traveled about to destroy the Church who appeared unto them?

A.  An angel of the Lord.

18 Q.  For what purpose?

A.  To warn them of their sins and to tell them to cease from evil.

19 Q.  What were the names of Mosiah's sons?

A.  Ammon, Aaron, Omner and Himni.

20 Q.  After Alma and his friends were convinced of their sins what did they do?

A.  They preached the word of God amid great trials.

21 Q.  To whom did Mosiah deliver the plates, interpreters, and other precious things?

A.  To Alma, the son of Alma.

22 Q.  When Aaron, Mosiah's son, refused to be king, what did the people do at the suggestion of Mosiah?

A. They elected judges to rule over them.

23 Q. To what positions was the younger Alma appointed?

A. To be the high priest and first chief judge.

24 Q. When did the reign of the kings cease?

A. At Mosiah's death, five hundred and nine years after Lehi left Jerusalem.

25 Q. Who was brought before Alma in the first year of his judgeship for teaching priestcraft?

A. Nehor.

26 Q. What was it he taught that was wrong?

A. He said that all mankind should be saved regardless of their sins, and that priests and teachers should not labor with their hands.

27 Q. When Gideon, who had delivered Limhi's people from bondage, withstood him, what did Nehor do to him?

A. He slew him with the sword.

28 Q. What was done with the murderer?

A. He suffered death according to the law.

29 Q. What man after the order of Nehor afterwards arose and began to lead away many people?

A. Amlici.

30 Q. What did his followers do?

A. They chose him to be their king.

31 Q. When he had gained this position what wicked act did he perform?

A. He stirred up his people to war against the supporters of the republic.

32 Q. In the battle which followed who were victorious?

A. The people of the republic.

33 Q. When the Amlicites had fled what did they next do?

A. They united with the Lamanites and returned to fight.

34 Q. How were they distinguished from the Nephites?

A. By a red mark which they placed on their foreheads.

35 Q. Why did they do this?

A. That God's word might be fulfilled when He said to Nephi: "I will set a mark upon him that fighteth against thee and thy seed."

36 Q.   Who were victorious in this great battle?

A.   The people of God.

37 Q.   What became of Amlici?

A.   Alma contended with and slew him.

38 Q.   After this was peace established?

A.   Not until another battle had been fought.

39 Q.   Why did the Lord permit His people to be thus afflicted?

A.   That they might be humble and seek him more diligently.

—◦▶◀◦—

## CHAPTER XI.

ALMA'S LABORS AS HIGH PRIEST—AMULEK ASSISTS HIM
—ZEEZROM'S UNBELIEF—DESTRUCTION OF AMMONIHAH
—AMMON'S LABORS AMONG THE LAMANITES—CONVERTS THE KING, QUEEN AND OTHERS.

1 Q.   Who was Nephihah?

A.   A man appointed by Alma to be Chief Judge.

2 Q.   Why did Alma resign this position?

A.   That he might have more time as High Priest to teach the people their duties.

3 Q.   In what condition were the people at this time?

A.   There began to be much wickedness among them.

4 Q.   How did Alma preach to the people?

A.   He told them plainly of their sins and urged them to repent.

5 Q.   Those who received his words accepted what ordinance?

A.   That of baptism.

6 Q.   What treatment did Alma receive in the city of Ammonihah?

A.   The people reviled and spit upon him, and cast him out of their city.

7 Q. When he was about to leave the place forever, what occurred?

A. An angel of the Lord came and told him to return.

8 Q. Who received, fed him and afterwards became his companion in the ministry?

A. Amulek.

9 Q. How had this man been turned from his evil ways?

A. Through the visitation of an angel.

10 Q. While these men were speaking to the people who sought to confuse them?

A. Those versed in law, principal among whom was Zeezrom.

11 Q. Did Zeezrom remain unbelieving?

A. No, the testimony of Alma and Amulek convinced him of his sins.

12 Q. When the people became angry at these holy men what did Zeezrom do?

A. He acknowledged his sins and plead for them.

13 Q. What was done with him?

A. He was cast out.

14 Q. What afterwards became of him?

A. He was healed of a fever and was then baptized.

15 Q. What was done with Alma and Amulek?

A. They were bound with strong cords.

16 Q. What sad scene were they then forced to witness?

A. The martyrdom by fire of many who had believed their words, and the burning of the holy scriptures.

17 Q. What was then done with these righteous men?

A. They were cast into prison.

18 Q. After many days, when many had met in the prison to revile them, what occurred?

A. The bonds were burst, and the prison walls fell, burying the wicked who were within, and permitting Alma and Amulek to go forth unharmed.

19 Q. When the people heard the noise and saw these men coming forth what did they do?

A. They fled with great fear.

20 Q.   Where did Alma and his companion then go and establish a church?

A.   In the land of Sidom.

21 Q.   What sacrifice did Amulek make by leaving Ammonihah?

A.   He was deprived of all his wealth.

22 Q.   From Sidom whence did these two go?

A.   To Alma's home in Zarahemla.

23 Q.   What happened to the city of Ammonihah in the year after it was visited by Alma?

A.   The Lamanites destroyed the city and every one of the inhabitants.

24 Q.   In what condition were the people of Nephi at the end of the fourteenth year of the reign of the Judges?

A.   They received and obeyed the word of God with gladness.

25 Q.   What had become of the four sons of Mosiah who received the truth when Alma did?

A.   They had been preaching the word of God for fourteen years to the Lamanites.

26 Q.   Where did Alma meet them after their absence?

A.   In the land of Gideon as they were on their way to Zarahemla.

27 Q.   When these men had first reached the lands of the Lamanites how did they begin their labors?

A.   By separating and going to different parts.

28 Q.   Who went to the land of Ishmael?

A.   Ammon, who seems to have been the leader.

29 Q.   When bound and taken before king Lamoni how was he treated?

A.   He gained favor with the king and became his servant?

30 Q.   How was Ammon's power shown forth just after entering the king's service?

A.   By contending with some Lamanites who sought to scatter the king's flocks.

31 Q.   How was Ammon preserved from harm?

A.   By the power of God, for the Lord promised Mosiah that his sons should not be harmed.

32 Q. After Lamoni's servants had testified of Ammon's great power who did the king say that he was?

A. The Great Spirit.

33 Q. What astonished the king still more?

A. When Ammon came into his presence, and discerned the thoughts of his heart.

34 Q. When Ammon had preached the gospel to the king, what was the result?

A. Lamoni believed, and fell to the earth, as if he were dead, under the power of God.

35 Q. How long was he in this condition?

A. Two days and two nights.

36 Q. What were the king's feelings when he arose?

A. His joy was full, because of the things revealed to him.

37 Q. Who were then overcome by the Spirit?

A. The king, queen, Ammon and the servants of the king, except one woman named Abish.

38 Q. Who was this woman?

A. A Lamanite, who had been converted to the Lord for many years.

39 Q. What did she do on seeing these things?

A. She went from house to house with the news.

40 Q. When one wicked man would have slain Ammon, what happened?

A. He fell dead.

41 Q. When there was about to be a contention among those who had assembled how was it prevented?

A. By those who had fallen being raised again, and declaring the joy they felt.

# CHAPTER XII.

AMMON DELIVERS HIS BROTHERS FROM PRISON—KING LAMONI RECEIVES THE TRUTH—MANY CONVERTS MADE —REFUSE TO FIGHT—EMIGRATE TO LAND OF ZARAHEMLA—KORIHOR'S FALSE DOCTRINE AND FATE—APOSTASY OF ZORAMITES.

1 Q. After a church had been established among Lamoni's people whither was Ammon told to go?

A. To the land of Middoni.

2 Q. For what purpose?

A. To deliver from prison his brethren Aaron, Muloki and Ammah.

3 Q. Why did Lamoni insist upon going with him?

A. To try and find favor with the king of Middoni, Antiomno, and have these men released.

4 Q. As they were journeying thither whom did they meet?

A. Lamoni's father, who was king over all the land, including Middoni.

5 Q. How did he feel?

A. He was angry and sought to slay Lamoni.

6 Q. How was he prevented?

A. By Ammon, who also overpowered the king.

7 Q. On what conditions was his life spared?

A. That he would permit Ammon's brethren to be freed, and Lamoni to retain his kingdom and act as he desired.

8 Q. When the old king was softened what more did he desire?

A. That Ammon and his brethren should visit him in his kingdom.

9 Q. In what condition were Ammon's brethren delivered?

A. They were naked, and sore from much suffering.

10 Q. What kind of a people did Aaron and his brothers find in Jerusalem and the region where they went to labor?

A. A very hard-hearted people.

-11 Q. How were these holy men directed in all their travels and labors?

A. By the Spirit of God.

12 Q. While Ammon taught Lamoni's people whither did Aaron and his brothers go?

A. To Lamoni's father, in the land of Nephi.

13 Q. How were they received by the king?

A. With great kindness.

14 Q. What was the effect of their teachings?

A. The king and his household were converted to the truth.

15 Q. How did the king assist these men in their work?

A. By sending forth a decree that they should be unmolested.

16 Q. What was characteristic of those Lamanites who received the gospel?

A. They remained faithful to the end.

17 Q. What name did these numerous converts adopt?

A. Anti-Nephi-Lehies.

18 Q. When the unconverted Lamanites prepared to fight their brethren, what course did the latter pursue?

A. They buried their weapons of war in testimony that they would no more shed blood.

19 Q. What did they do when they went forth to meet their enemies?

A. They prostrated themselves to the earth and called on the name of God.

20 Q. After their enemies had slain one thousand and five what did they do?

A. They threw down their weapons, and many became converted to the truth.

21 Q. Why did none of the Amalekites or Amulonites, but only actual descendants of Laman and Lemuel receive the truth?

A. Because the former had been once in the church, and having fallen away had become hardened in sin.

22 Q. Why were the descendants of Amulon afterwards hunted by the Lamanites?

A. To fulfill the words of Abinadi, whom Amulon and the other priests had martyred.

23 Q. As the people of Anti-Nephi-Lehi were continually being persecuted by the Lamanites what did the Lord command them through Ammon to do?

A. To go to the land of Zarahemla.

24 Q. What part of the land was assigned to this people?

A. The part called Jershon.

25 Q. On what condition did the Nephites place their armies to protect these brethren?

A. That they would give part of their substance to maintain the armies.

26 Q. In the seventeenth year of the reign of the Judges who commenced to teach false doctrine?

A. Korihor, who was anti-Christ.

27 Q. What was the law at this time concerning a man's belief?

A. Each could believe as he desired, and was only punished for crimes committed.

28 Q. What did he teach?

A. That the doctrines of the gospel were false, and that the people were in bondage to their leaders.

29 Q. When contending with Alma what did he command?

A. A sign.

30 Q. What sign was given him?

A. He was struck dumb.

31 Q. What did he then acknowledge?

A. That the devil had appeared to him in the form of an angel and had deceived him.

32 Q. What was his fate for perverting the ways of the Lord?

A. He went begging from house to house until he was trampled upon and killed.

33 Q. After Korihor's power was ended of whose apostasy did Alma hear?

A.  That part of the people called Zoramites led by Zoram.
34 Q.  Where did these apostates gather?
A.  In Antionum, between the land of Jershon and a wilderness occupied by the Lamanites.
35 Q.  What were the means employed to try and reclaim this people?
A.  The preaching of the gospel.
36 Q.  Whom did Alma take with him to perform this labor?
A.  Ammon, Aaron, Omner, Amulek, Zeezrom, and two of his own sons.
37 Q.  What astonished these men when they came to the land of the Zoramites?
A.  To find that synagogues were built where the people worshiped one day every week in a strange way.
38 Q.  In what did this worship consist?
A.  Each one who desired to worship must ascend a pulpit erected in the middle of the synagogue, stretch his hands towards heaven, and offer a prepared prayer.
39 Q.  What were Alma's feelings on seeing this?
A.  He was sorrowful and prayed mightily to God.
40 Q.  When he and his companions were filled with the Holy Spirit, according to his prayer, what did they do?
A.  They separated and commenced to preach.
41 Q.  Who alone came to hear and believed their teachings?
A.  The poor who were cast out of the synagogues because of their coarse apparel.
42 Q.  When Alma and his companions had withdrawn to the land of Jershon, what did the Zoramites do with those who had believed the truth?
A.  They drove them thither also.
43 Q.  What did the unbelieving Zoramites do?
A.  They mixed with the Lamanites and stirred them up to war against the Nephites.

2

# CHAPTER XIII.

ALMA AND HIS SONS GO FORTH TO PREACH—ALMA IS TAK-
EN AWAY—AMALICKIAH'S WICKEDNESS—MORONI'S
LABORS TO PRESERVE HIS PEOPLE—THE REMARKABLE
TWO THOUSAND.

1 Q. WHAT did Alma do on seeing the iniquities among the people?

A. He called his sons, gave each a charge and sent them forth to preach.

2 Q. To which son did he deliver the plates of Nephi?

A. Helaman.

3 Q. What was he to do with them?

A. Whatsoever the Lord commanded him.

✗ 4 Q. Which one of the sons of Alma went somewhat astray?

A. Corianton.

5 Q. How did his father say he could alone receive eternal happiness?

A. By repentance and being faithful to the end.

6 Q. What did Alma tell him concerning the resurrection?

A. A time should come when all the dead should rise.

7 Q. Between death and the resurrection where should the souls of men be?

A. The righteous in a state of rest and the wicked in one of misery.

8 Q. What is to be the final condition of the souls of men?

A. The good shall shine in God's kingdom and the others shall be without.

9 Q. Did Alma's sons alone go forth to preach?

A. No, he also went, being unable to rest at home.

10 Q. What object did the Lamanites and Zoramites have in coming to war against the Nephites in the eighteenth year of the Judges?

A. They desired to gain power and rule over them.

11 Q. How did the two armies compare in size?

A. That of the Lamanites was more than double the size of the opposing force.

12 Q. What was God's command to the Nephites in regard to going to war?

A. If they were not guilty of either the first or second offense, then they were to defend themselves.

13 Q. In the severe battle who were victors?

A. Moroni, the Nephite commander, and his hosts.

14 Q. What promise were the Lamanites forced to make?

A. That they would come to war no more against the Nephites.

15 Q. What became of Alma?

A. He started as if to go to the land of Melek and was never heard of more.

16 Q. What was the belief concerning his end?

A. That he was taken in the Spirit unto God.

17 Q. What did he tell his son Helaman concerning the Nephites?

A. That they should dwindle in unbelief.

18 Q. Whom did he bless?

A. All that should remain faithful.

19 Q. What wickedness did Amalickiah seek to bring about among the Nephites?

A. To lead them astray and to make himself their king.

20 Q. When Moroni discovered his design to bring the people into bondage, what did he do?

A. He went among the people and urged them to defend their liberties and homes.

21 Q. What became of Amalickiah when he saw the forces Moroni had collected to oppose him?

A. He fled and joined the Lamanites.

22 Q. What did he then seek to do?

A. To stir the Lamanites up to war against the Nephites.

23 Q. Was he successful?

A. Not at first, as a part only were willing to go to battle.

24 Q. How did he succeed in becoming king of the Lamanites?

A. By the murder of the king.

25 Q. What means did he then adopt to get the people to go to war?

A. He appointed men to speak unto them from their towers and urge them to do so.

26 Q. What means did Moroni adopt to protect his brethren from their enemies?

A. By the construction of earth-works and forts around each city.

27 Q. What blessings did the faithfulness of the Nephites bring upon them during these troublous times?

A. Prosperity and happiness.

28 Q. When Morianton began to stir up confusion among part of the people in the twenty-fourth year, what did he try to do?

A. To lead the disaffected ones to the land northward.

29 Q. How was he prevented?

A. By Moroni sending an army, which captured and brought them back.

30 Q. What caused the next disturbance among the Nephites?

A. The desire of some to dispense with judges and have a king.

31 Q. Even after the majority had decided against having kings, what had to be done in order to prepare the people to meet the Lamanites who were coming against them?

A. Many had to be slain; the others then yielded.

32 Q. What success did Amalickiah and his wicked hosts have in the beginning of the war?

A. They captured many fortified cities.

33 Q. When did Ammoron become king of the Lamanites?

A. After Amalickiah had been slain while asleep by Teancum, a Nephite commander.

34 Q. What remarkable body of men fought in this war?

A. Two thousand and sixty young men, sons of the people of Ammon.

35 Q. What success attended them?

A. They fought with great valor, and though some were wounded none were killed.

36 Q. Why was this?

A. Because of their exceeding great faith in God and His power to deliver them.

37 Q. Who had taught them to have faith?

A. Their mothers.

---

# CHAPTER XIV.

REBELLION AMONG THE NEPHITES—GADIANTON ROBBERS—NEPHI AND LEHI PREACH—PRISON WALLS SHAKE—SAMUEL, THE LAMANITE—HIS WARNINGS—GREAT COMMOTIONS IN THE EARTH—JESUS APPEARS—INSTRUCTS PEOPLE AND CHOOSES APOSTLES.

1 Q. To whom did Moroni write a letter of censure because of not sending provisions and men to the assistance of his army?

A. Pahoran, chief judge in Zarahemla.

2 Q. What reason did Pahoran give for his apparent neglect?

A. That some of the Nephites had revolted and driven him from his judgment seat.

3 Q. How did Moroni end the rebellion?

A. He took part of his force and gathered all he could on his way to Zarahemla, where he overcame the rebels and slew all who persisted in opposition.

4 Q. After this, what success attended the Nephites in their wars?

A. They conquered the Lamanites, whose king was slain.

5 Q. In the thirty-seventh and eighth years whither did many of the Nephites emigrate?

A. Into the land northward, now called North America.

6 Q. Who was Kishkumen?

A.  A murderer who was leader of a wicked secret order, afterwards known as Gadianton Robbers.

7 Q.  What did these robbers do?

A.  They plundered and murdered.

8 Q.  When the people began to apostatize because of their prosperity, who went forth to preach?

A.  Nephi and Lehi, sons of Helaman.

9 Q.  What success attended them?

A.  By the power of God that was with them they converted many Lamanites and apostate Nephites.

10 Q.  When cast into prison by the Lamanites what miracle converted their opposers?

A.  Nephi and Lehi appeared to be encircled by fire, their prison walls shook, and a still, small voice whispered repentance into the ears of the unconverted.

11 Q.  What did these persons do when convinced?

A.  They went among the people and declared the truth.

12 Q.  In what did the Lamanites begin to excel the Nephites?

A.  In righteousness.

13 Q.  What was done with the Gadianton Robbers?

A.  The Lamanites drove them from their midst, but the Nephites supported and built them up.

14 Q.  What mighty man did God preserve to warn the people of troubles unless they would repent?

A.  Nephi, who was assisted by Lehi.

15 Q.  How did the Lord bring the people to repentance?

A.  By causing a famine through all the land.

16 Q.  After repenting and again becoming sinful what means were used to stir them up to remembrance?

A.  The Gadianton Robbers were used as a scourge.

17 Q.  Whom did the Lord send from among the Lamanites to warn the people of impending destruction?

A.  Samuel, a Lamanite prophet.

18 Q.  Of what other great event did he prophesy?

A.  The coming of Christ in five years.

19 Q.  After Samuel had delivered his message and the wicked sought to take him, whither did he go?

A. To his own country and people.

20 Q. What became of the holy man Nephi?

A. He departed, but whither he went no man knew.

21 Q. In which year of the reign of the Judges was the sign of the Savior's birth given?

A. The ninety-second.

22 Q. From this time how did the Nephites reckon their years?

A. From the time the sign was given.

23 Q. What change came' over the Lamanites who accepted the truth?

A. Their skin became white.

24 Q. Why were the Gadianton Robbers permitted to harass the Nephites soon after the sign?

A. Because the latter became careless and wicked.

25 Q. How were they enabled to overcome their enemies?

A. By humbling themselves before the Lord.

26 Q. In what condition were the people in the thirtieth year?

A. Great inequality existed, and all manner of evils abounded.

27 Q. How were the people warned to repent?

A. By holy prophets, among whom was Nephi, the son of him of whose death no account is given.

28 Q. What great event occurred in the thirty-fourth year, in the first month and in the fourth day of the month?

A. A dense darkness commenced which lasted three days.

29 Q. During this time of darkness what happened?

A. The face of the whole land became changed through storms and earthquakes.

30 Q. Why were many cities destroyed?

A. Because of the wickedness of the inhabitants.

31 Q. How were those who were spared urged to repentance and faithfulness?

A. By the voice of the Savior from heaven.

32 Q. Of what were all these things the sign?

A. The death of the Messiah.

33 Q.   While a great multitude were gathered about the temple at Bountiful, after these events, who came from heaven and stood in their midst?

A.   Jesus Christ, the Son of God.

34 Q.   What did He tell them to do so they might know He was the Lord?

A.   To feel His wounds.

35 Q.   Upon whom did Jesus confer the power to baptize?

A.   Upon Nephi and eleven other good men.

36 Q.   What did He send them forth to declare?

A.   That all must repent and be baptized or they could not be saved.

37 Q.   After Jesus had given much instruction and healed the sick, what became of Him?

A.   A cloud overshadowed Him and He went to heaven.

38 Q.   When a great multitude assembled the next day to see the Savior, who were baptized?

A.   Nephi and his brethren of the twelve.

39 Q.   What followed this?

A.   They received the Holy Ghost and the ministrations of the Savior and His angels.

40 Q.   How did the faith of the Nephites compare with that of the saints in the Old World?

A.   It was greater.

41 Q.   What principles and ordinances did the Savior give to His followers on this land?

A.   The same as those taught at Jerusalem.

# CHAPTER XV.

CHURCH ORGANIZED—PROMISES OF THE SAVIOR TO HIS
APOSTLES—PEOPLE BEGIN TO FALL IN UNBELIÉF—
MORMON'S CALLING—MORONI'S LABORS—THE JARED-
ITES—THIER ORIGIN—TRAVELS—TROUBLES—DESTRUC-
TION.

1 Q. How long did Jesus teach the people at His second visit?

A. Three days.

2 Q. What was the Church called which the apostles organized?

A. The Church of Christ.

3 Q. Who appeared to the apostles at one time while they were fasting and praying?

A. The Savior.

4 Q. What did the Lord promise nine of the apostles in accordance with their wishes?

A. "Therefore, after that ye are seventy and two years old, ye shall come unto me in my kingdom, and with me ye shall find rest."

5 Q. What wish of the remaining three did he promise to fulfill?

A. That they should live on earth without pain until Christ should come in glory, and then be changed to immortality.

6 Q. What other blessing was promised these three?

A. They should be able to bring many to the truth.

7 Q. What peculiar characteristic of the early Church caused the Lord to bless all the members?

A. They were so united as to hold all things common among them.

8 Q. In what year did pride begin to cause a change in this
respect?

A. In the two hundred and first year.

9 Q. What was the result of this change?

A. Apostates became numerous, Gadianton Robbers were
again active and the true Church was persecuted.

10 Q. After three hundred and twenty years, when Ammaron
hid the plates, to whom did he tell the place of
hiding?

A. Mormon, who was then ten years of age.

11 Q. At what age was he to get, and engrave what he had
seen upon the plates of Nephi?

A. Twenty-four.

12 Q. When terrible wars began to occur who was appointed
leader of the Nephite armies?

A. Mormon, who was only sixteen years old.

13 Q. Why was it that disaster generally attended the Nephites?

A. Because they were guilty of wickedness.

14 Q. Why did Mormon refuse to be their leader longer?

A. Because after they had won some battles they boasted
in their own strength and swore by the most holy
things that they would conquer their enemies.

15 Q. When Mormon afterwards did assume command what
were his feelings?

A. He was without hope of success because his people
were so wicked.

16 Q. What followed when Mormon had gathered all his
people at the hill Cumorah, in the year 384,
A. D.?

A. A battle in which all the Nephites were slain except
twenty-four, among whom were Mormon and his
son Moroni.

17 Q. Who finished Mormon's record?

A. Moroni, who afterwards hid it up.

18 Q. When did he prophesy that the record should be
revealed?

A. In a day of secret combinations and great wickedness.

19 Q. Of what people does Moroni give an account as being destroyed in the north country?

A. The Jaredites, who came from the tower of Babel.

20 Q. How was their record obtained?

A. From twenty-four plates found by the people of Limhi and called the book of Ether.

21 Q. Through whose influence was the language of Jared and company saved from confusion, and they led to this highly-favored land?

A. The brother of Jared, a man of mighty faith.

22 Q. How did they cross the mighty waters?

A. In eight water-tight barges.

23 Q. How did the Lord prepare sixteen small stones, which had been molten out of rock, to furnish light?

A. By touching them with His finger.

24 Q. While in a high mount what did Jared's brother effect through his great faith?

A. He saw, not only the finger with which the stones were touched, but the Lord's whole person.

25 Q. How long were these people on the water?

A. Three hundred and forty-four days, when the promised land was reached.

26 Q. What did the people desire of their leaders before they died?

A. They desired a king.

27 Q. When Jared's brother vainly tried to move them from this purpose, whom did they choose?

A. Orihah, a son of Jared, after all the other sons of Jared and his brother had refused the position.

28 Q. What began to exist shortly after the kingdom was established?

A. Divisions, secret organizations and strifes.

29 Q. How did the Lord warn them to repent of their sins?

A. He sent prophets unto them.

30 Q. What afflictions followed when these warnings were unheeded?

A. Famine and poisonous serpents were sent.

31 Q. How did they find relief from these?

A. By humbling themselves before God.

32 Q. What is said in this record concerning the lands northward and southward, or North and South America?

A. North America was covered with inhabitants and South America was preserved as a wilderness to get game.

33 Q. What kind of people were the inhabitants?

A. They were very industrious and skillful.

34 Q. Who was Ether?

A. A prophet of God who was sent to warn the people in the days of Coriantumr.

35 Q. When the people cast him out because of his prophecies, where did he dwell?

A. In the cavity of a rock.

36 Q. What was Ether's prediction to Coriantumr?

A. That if he would repent his family and kingdom should be spared to him, otherwise, he alone should be spared to see Ether's prediction fulfilled.

37 Q. Did the king repent?

A. No; and as a result wars began to increase among all the people.

38 Q. After millions were slain where did the remnants meet for the last great battle?

A. At the hill Ramah, afterwards called Cumorah.

39 Q. What two men closed the struggle of the two armies by fighting to the death?

A. Coriantumr, one leader, and Shiz, the other.

40 Q. Who went and viewed the great work of destruction?

A. Ether, whom God preserved to finish the record.

# CHAPTER XVI.

INSTRUCTIONS TO CHURCH MEMBERS—INFANT BAPTISM—
HOW TO KNOW IF THE BOOK OF MORMON IS TRUE—
MORONI'S EXHORTATION—JOSEPH SMITH'S TESTIMONY.

1 Q. What does Moroni in this book say the Lamanites
did with every Nephite they captured who would
not deny Christ?

A. Each was put to death.

2 Q. How did Moroni escape?

A. By keeping himself concealed.

3 Q. How are we informed that Jesus imparted the Holy
Ghost to His disciples?

A. By the laying on of hands.

4 Q. Who else were set apart by the laying on of hands?

A. The various officers of the Church.

5 Q. Besides the first ordinances of the gospel, what is
fully explained in the book of Moroni.

A. The manner of administering the sacrament.

6 Q. To whom was baptism administered?

A. Only to such as "brought forth fruit meet that they
were worthy of it."

7 Q. How many witnesses were necessary to condemn an
iniquitous person?

A. Three.

8 Q. When Church members committed sin how did they
obtain forgiveness?

A. By earnestly repenting.

9 Q. What does Moroni say concerning a gift grudgingly
given?

A. It profiteth a man nothing.

10 Q. And when one shall pray without real intent of heart?

A. It is counted evil unto him.

11 Q.  Whence come all good and all evil?
 A.  All good from God, and the evil from Satan.
12 Q.  How can every man know good from evil?
 A.  By "the Spirit of Christ" which is given him.
13 Q.  How can all good gifts be obtained?
 A.  Through the exercise of faith.
14 Q.  What other two qualities are we exhorted to cultivate?
 A.  Hope and charity.
15 Q.  What does Mormon say in a letter to Moroni respecting the baptism of little children?
 A.  That such is solemn mockery before God.
16 Q.  Why is this?
 A.  Because baptism is for the remission of sins, and little children are free from sin.
17 Q.  To what depths does Mormon inform us the Nephites descended before their destruction?
 A.  So low that they devoured the flesh of their enemies whom they slew in war.
18 Q.  How does Moroni say people can learn of the truth of the Book of Mormon?
 A.  By asking God, with a sincere heart, in the name of Christ.
19 Q.  What is Moroni's last exhortation to all people?
 A.  To come unto Christ, and lay hold upon every good gift.
20 Q.  What is the testimony of the Prophet Joseph concerning the Book of Mormon?
 A.  "I told the brethren that the Book of Mormon was the most correct of any book on earth, and the keystone of our religion, and a man would get nearer to God by abiding by its precepts, than by any other book."